Milly, Mo
and the Train

"We may look different but we feel the same."

Milly and Molly dawdled along in the sun. Suddenly, they heard the rumble of a train.

"Come on, you'll miss it," shouted Molly.
Milly ran as fast as she could to catch up.
"No I won't." she said.

They reached the Railway Bridge just as the train snaked around the hill and came towards them.

"I see it," cried Molly.
"I saw it first," puffed Milly.

High in the blue sky above the train,
a small plane drew a soft white line.

"That's magic," said Milly.
Molly just nodded.

The rumble of the train grew louder and louder. So loud, it rumbled in Milly and Molly's chests.

As it came straight towards them,
they wanted to run.

Suddenly, the engine driver blew two hoots on the whistle and he waved.

Milly and Molly waved back wildly, jumping up and down as they did.

They raced to the other side of the bridge to watch the train snake away.

The rumble of the train disappeared, leaving behind a cloud of filthy garbage.

"Disgusting," said Milly and Molly together.
"Come on, let's pick it up."

And they did.

The last piece of garbage looked more like a parcel. It was heavy.

"It's money," said Milly, as she tore off the wrapping paper.
"It's stacks of money," shrieked Molly, as her legs went wobbly.
"There's too much to keep," sighed Milly.

Milly and Molly took turns carrying the heavy parcel of money, and the garbage, to the Police Station.

"Hello! Hello! Hello! What have we got here then?" inquired the policeman.
"We found all this money by the train track," stammered Milly.
"We were picking up the garbage," Molly added.

"Well done," beamed the policeman. "How would you like to be rewarded?"

"I know," gasped Milly and Molly together. "We'd like a plane to go up in the sky and and write, "Don't litter."

The next day Milly and Molly stood with the policeman on the Railway Bridge.

High in the sky, for all the world to see,
were the words *don't litter*.

The train driver hooted and waved. And as the rumble of the train disappeared, there wasn't one piece of garbage to be seen.